Sufism
The Reality
of
Religion

Molana Salaheddin Ali Nader Shah Angha
"Pir Oveyssi"

 M.T.O. Shahmaghsoudi® Publications

M.T.O. Shahmaghsoudi® Publications

Molana Salaheddin Ali Nader Shah Angha, *"Pir Oveyssi"*

Sufism
The Reality of Religion

Library of Congress Catalog Card Number: 98-060034
ISBN: 0-910735-80-8

Printed in the U.S.A.

Published by M.T.O. Shahmaghsoudi
Printing and Publication Center
10590 Magnolia Ave., Suite G
Riverside, CA 92505
U.S.A.

e-mail: angha_rs@pacbell.net

M.T.O. Shahmaghsoudi Headquarters
5225 Wisconsin Ave., N.W., Suite 502
Washington, D.C. 20015
U.S.A.

e-mail: mtos@cais.com
website: http://mto.shahmaghsoudi.org

Other books in the Sufism Lecture Series:

Sufism

Sufism and Wisdom

Sufism and Islam

Sufism and Peace

Sufism and Knowledge

CONTENTS

Note On Translation And Transliteration

In translating from the Persian, the masculine gender is used in references to God and human being *("ensan")*. This is partly for convenience but also because the Persian language has no distinct gender denominations; thus, the Persian pronoun *"ou"* may mean *"he"* as well as *"she"* with the proper meaning contextually determined.

INTRODUCTION

In November 27, 1996, I had the great honor of meeting His Holiness Molana Salaheddin Ali Nader Shah Angha when he came to the German Institute for Middle East Studies in Hamburg. The experience of meeting Hazrat Pir and listening to his lecture had a lasting influence on my outlook and personal life.

The German Institute for Middle East Studies is involved with the political and economic issues relating to the Islamic world. Hazrat Pir was kind enough to meet with me and my staff privately to discuss these issues, during which time he showed us new approaches in viewing social, political, and religious issues. I found his perspective on these issues not only unique, but applicable in resolving some of the most fundamental problems facing societies today.

Religion has not always made the world more peaceful. Throughout history, people have been tempted to misuse religion and its so-called "eternal truths" to justify the use of violence to achieve political ends. This phenomenon continues today, appearing especially in the cradle of the three monotheistic religions, the Middle East, where it is a bitter daily reality.

Humans around the world today are more closely connected than ever before. The somewhat abstract term "globalization" has become a concrete reality in the everyday lives of individuals, nations and states. With global trade, economics have bound us together inextricably. Electronic communications have familiarized individuals with the activities, customs, traditions and ideas of peoples around the world.

In contrast to this phenomenon of economic and social globalization, political life in many countries is becoming increasingly focused on the separation of states and nations by strict and unchangeable borders. Nevertheless, political decisions in any one state inevitably affect us all. This especially becomes a concern when such decisions include violence or warfare. In an effort to help avoid these destructive choices, numerous regional and international organizations have devoted themselves to promoting conflict management and conflict resolution among states. It is important that all people realize their common responsibility in making our world a peaceful one, and keep this responsibility in mind when choosing a course of action.

With globalization and consumerism, many have succumbed to the seemingly unlimited possibilities offered by ever-expanding markets and economic opportunities. Particularly in the West, materialistic thinking has led to a greatly diminished focus on the intellectual and spiritual dimensions of human existence. The "autonomous" human being, detached from all ties to any Supreme Reality or life in the hereafter, has become the Western ideal. However, in reality, this focus on autonomy has imposed huge and conflicting pressures on the individuals who subscribe to it. On one hand, the natural sciences have enabled them to be masters of nature. On the other hand, these individuals must live in fear of what their mastery of nature has created, whether it is the nuclear bomb with its sudden and violent effects, or the slow, creeping destruction wrought by pollution and the pillaging of nature's treasures. This tension is felt not just by Westerners, but by all people who have devoted themselves to a materialistic reshaping of the world and are now helplessly caught in its clutches.

In the face of this dilemma, individuals from all parts of the world have begun to search for a way to escape the dead end. They seek a path that can satisfy the undeniable material needs of a swiftly growing human population while also providing the space and freedom for people to recognize themselves in the fullness of their being. In other words, all humans need to realize their existence as individuals, as part of the human race, and as an element of a universe in which the true senses transcend the mere fulfillment of material needs. If there is one quest that will determine the future fate of humanity, then it is the search for this path toward self-realization.

The question remains as to whether the major global religions will be able to take on the challenge of guiding humanity toward this goal. Will they be able to reveal to the individual the path that will guide him/her to be in harmony with existence itself and allow him / her to confidently and freely determine his/her own life? Unfortunately, the world's dominant religions are giant structures, separated from one another be dogmatic systems and often competing for new followers. They have seemed more concerned with these issues than with the interests of their individual members.

Recently, there has been talk of an ecumenical movement which would foster communication between these religions. This movement focuses on the value of the texts which each religion has passed down through the generations containing the teachings of the great Prophets, including Muhammad, Jesus, Buddha, and Moses. These texts are indispensable to mankind. Throughout history, humans have searched for ways to overcome the many limits to their existence: their bonds to a people or ethnic group, their limitation by state borders, the stubbornness of the religious statutes of their belief systems, and their own physical vulnerabilities. The words of the Prophets are not like religious buildings, where only "believers" are permitted to enter and benefit. Instead, they offer to all people signs and clues of the reality in which human and humanity, creature and creator, diversity and oneness, become one. Knowledge of this reality does not come through blind adherence to written texts or to the traditions of people or institutions. Instead, it comes by following the path of cognition. It begins with that which is nearest to a person: one's self. Although this self is very close, the realization that it offers can only be acquired through a long journey. It is at the end of this journey that the individual recognizes that the true "Self" is one and the same as Absolute Existence.

Modern humans have turned to the guarantee of "human rights" as their best protection against violence and injustice. However, no external, political policy can provide the confirmation of human dignity that is inherent in the realization of the true "Self". This confirmation of a person's freedom and right to justice, and the rejection of any injustice as a deep injury to universal "Existence", are the best and most solid foundations on which to build a system of human rights. Only with such a system can universal justice truly be realized.

A new world order based on these foundations would transcend the existing order, which is dominated by long-established state and religious systems. It would meet the need--brought on by the race of global networking-- for new thinking, new, more inherent forms of recognition, and new methods of state and social organization. It would appeal for the just distribution of all resources, without regard to ethnic, religious, or state affiliations. At the same time, it would demand that nature and the environment be treated in accordance with the respect that human dignity demands. Faced with the threat of worldwide destruction, humanity can no longer do without the stable and lasting peace this new system offers.

In the insightful treatise you are about to read, Hazrat Pir explains how the path to cognition of one's true "Self" is the only way to overcome the tension between the development of human beings and their fear of being destroyed by their own striving.

Dr. Udo Steinbach
October, 1997

Professor Udo Steinbach has been the Director of the Deutsches Orient-Institut (German Institute for Middle East Studies) in Hamburg, Germany, since 1976. He is also Professor of Islamic Studies at the Hamburg University. He is the author of numerous articles and books dealing with the Middle East.

In God's Great Name

Before I begin, I would like to mention that the credibility of each person is based on presenting what belongs to him or her, and not repeating or reformulating what others have discovered, said, or done. I am neither an historian nor a "scholar." Therefore, I can only speak from my own personal discoveries and knowledge. For, as the philosopher Spinoza said, it is only that which we take hold of, demonstrate, and differentiate that has any reality.[1]

I speak from the perspective of Sufism in which I was born and raised--a heritage of 1400 years. Although I was brought up in a family where my great grandfather, grandfather and father had all been Masters of the Oveyssi School of Sufism, I was never

---

[1] For an introduction to the works of Spinoza, the reader is referred to Karl Jasper's book entitled *Spinoza*, from the Great Philosophers: The Original Thinkers series edited by Hannah Arendt and translated by Ralph Mannheim, New York: Harcourt Brace and Jovanovich, 1974.

allowed to think that because I was born and raised in the tradition, I knew it all. My father treated me like other students. He always said that spiritual learning and development is a matter of personal effort and discovery.

A widely prevalent belief holds that human beings are born into their religion. For example, adoption agencies who indicate an infant up for adoption is "Catholic" or "Protestant" or religious authorities who define a "Jew" as someone whose mother is Jewish. No one can inherit religion. Religion is the result of knowing God. With the grace of the Almighty God, my training began under the guidance of my grandfather and then continued under my father. To them I am forever grateful, for they did not allow my mind to deviate from the ultimate goal --reaching the Truth. My father always said, "The wise attract benefit and repel loss."

The Oveyssi School of Sufism dates back to the time of the Holy Prophet Muhammad (peace be upon him). The founder of the School is Hazrat Oveys Gharani[2], whose way of inward cognition was

---

[2] The conventional Arabic transliteration is *Uwais al-Qarani*.

approved by the Holy Prophet. The inspired and revealed spiritual knowledge has been passed down from the time of Hazrat Oveys to myself through an unbroken succession of Masters who are well known by historians and scholars.

Sufism is generally accepted to be the mystical dimension of Islam. Although the origin of Sufism has been variously explained and interpreted, I would like to present the way I have experienced it. Sufism is the reality of religion. By this I mean experiencing God in one's inner self, submitting to Him, and loving Him with one's mind, heart and soul, until no other but the Beloved remains. This is the reality of religion as I know it.

The word which captures the essence of Sufism is *irfan*, derived from the word *ma'rifa* which means "knowing." In this context, it means knowing God and being replete with divine knowledge or mysteries. It is the way of the Prophets. This is why I have defined Sufism as the reality of religion.

The urge to know is inherent in each human being. The quest for the meaning of life, for self-knowledge, for eternity, is timeless. It is not unique to

3

any particular race, creed, or culture, nor bound to any particular place. It is universal. As it is written in the Holy Qur'an (21:7): "Before you, also, the apostles We sent were but men, to whom We granted inspiration..."

Those for whom the quest for the ultimate Reality is the most important goal in life, and who do not give up their search until they discover the answer, are generally regarded as "mystics."

Mysticism is associated with mystery and the unknown. Often, it is associated with secret rites and special ceremonies for the initiated. Mysticism is the belief that union and absorption into God is possible through self-renunciation, contemplation and meditation. The mystical experience is considered to be one in which human reason has no part, being beyond human thinking or comprehension. In other words, it can only be known through personal experience. Therefore, the mind cannot grasp it and words cannot explain it. It is a mystery to those who have not had the experience. The mystical experience is usually associated with a sense of liberation, freedom, ecstasy, unity, contentment, abundance, compassion, knowledge, joy, and love.

4

The history of all religious traditions contains extensive accounts given by individuals who have undergone an experience that transcends the limitation of the senses. It is evident from these accounts that the intensity of the experience varies from one person to another. As these experiences come down to us they are frequently interpreted, formalized, ritualized and imitated. The true seeker, however, takes them as a signpost to persevere in his or her personal search for knowing the unknown. The seeker of God does not follow religion blindly, but searches for the truth within until the desired result is obtained.

The Prophets, Saints, and Enlightened can be considered the true models of the genuine mystical experience. Their voices heralding their long-sought answers echo in the silent books. In finding the answer, their lives and visions were transformed. And their voices reach the hearts of genuine seekers who rise to search for the truth of their being.

Sufism teaches that all knowledge is humanity's legacy, but that one does not receive it until one truly seeks it. And, until it is fully experienced in one's own lifetime, the reality of the message of each Prophet will never be known. My father, Hazrat Shah Maghsoud Sadegh Angha, describes humanity's basic conundrum as follows:

> Our own internal and spiritual ignorance causes neophytes not to try to know their true essence, which is the most sublime secret of nature. They are not even willing to discover and cognize their own essence. Instead, they always visualize an imaginary, far away goal, a goal which is ambiguous and unreal.[3]

In Islam, the quest for one's truth is called *qiyam* (rising), and it is central to the believer's daily life. This unflinching rising or unfaltering quest for truth is seen in the lives of the illustrious leaders of the various religious traditions. Buddha gave up his throne and kingdom and did not stop until he attained enlightenment. Despite the hardships Moses faced, he pursued his mission until he brought his people to the Promised Land. Jesus withstood with strength and endured the pain and suffering inflicted upon him because of his unswerving love for the Father. And Muhammad (peace and blessings be upon him) went

---

[3] Shah Maghsoud Sadegh Angha, *The Hidden Angles of Life*. Pomana, CA: Multidisciplinary Publications, 1975. The quote here is from a revision in preparation, p. 56.

on prolonged solitary meditation retreats (to the Cave of Hira) until God spoke to him, and afterwards his life was devoted to proclaiming the message of his Beloved.

Throughout time, people have attempted to express the ineffable quality of the mystical unity of all existence. These attempts appear in humanity's earliest sacred writings, as exemplified by the following quotations:

> *It moves, yet moves not.*
> *It is far, yet It is near.*
> *It is within all this.*
> *And yet without all this.*
>
> *The one Self never moves,*
> *yet is too swift for the mind.*
> *The senses cannot reach It.*
> *It is ever beyond their grasp.*
> *The Isha Upanishads* [4]
>
> *The Tao that can be told is not the eternal Tao.*
> *The name that can be named is not the eternal name.*
> *The nameless is the beginning of heaven and earth.*
> *The name is the mother of ten thousand things.*
> *The Tao Te Ching, Chapter One* [5]

---

[4] Shearer, A. and P. Russell, trans. *The Upanishads*. New York: Harper Colophon Books, 1978, p. 15.

This underlying unity has been the message of all the religious traditions named above. However, external circumstances and ignorance have caused the alienation and misunderstanding that has existed and still exists among their followers. When religion becomes institutionalized, through time it becomes ossified and takes on the characteristics of the surroundings in which it grows. Slowly, its reason for having sprung to life is covered with superstition, dogma, ignorance and prejudice. The vibrancy of the message is lost in interpretation, rituals and blind faith. The personal discovery of the "mystery", which was the core of the Prophets' beliefs and teachings, remains unknown to those who follow their words blindly.

In mathematics, we must first accept a basic premise or law before we can continue with the rest of our inquiry. If we do not accept that basic premise, we cannot go any further. This holds true in all investigative processes. If we do not accept a basic

---

[5] Lao Tsu, *Tao Te Ching*. New York: Vintage Books, 1972. Chapter One. Translated by Gia-Fu Feng and Jane English.,

law, nothing after that has any validity; there is no point of communality or agreement. If we do not fully understand a fundamental law, any answers we have are irrelevant and invalid, and that law has no enforcement capacity. Let me give you an example, told by my grandfather, Hazrat Mir Ghotbeddin. He said, "If you do not respect and trust the foundation and source of anything, how can you trust its results and product?" How can one deny the essence of that which has produced it and yet believe in the result?

People respond to God in much the same way. In religion, ritualization has superseded the acceptance of the preliminary law---God is Absolute and Ever-present. If we conceptualize this law as a tree, then the fruit of this tree must bear resemblance to the knowledge of that tree. The essence of the apple tree is its seed. The apple seed does not prove anything by growing, it simply manifests and fulfills the essence of the tree. The branches, leaves, flowers and fruits emanate from the essence and not vice versa. In the same spirit, the human being must manifest the divinity within in order to say that he or she is created in the image of God.

Paul Davies, the British physicist, has written about the world we have learned to think we see and the absoluteness of existence. He states that science is usually believed to be the basis for the construction of a picture of objective reality, of the external and physical world. With the advent of quantum theory, this vision of reality has disintegrated, and is being replaced by a revolutionary concept. Laboratory experiments have repeatedly demonstrated that atoms and subatomic particles, which are usually envisioned as minuscule little things, are not really things at all, not tiny separate specks of matter with a well-defined, independent existence.

Science is now demonstrating that reality is not a measurable property of the external world, but is instead intimately intertwined with our presence as observers and our own perception. Davies tells us that previous scientific "revolutions" had successively diminished the role of mankind from being the central player to a "...mere spectator of the cosmic drama." Quantum theory reinstates us, as observers, to the center of the stage, to the key role. "This idea implies that the universe only achieves a concrete existence as a result of this perception –it is created by its own inhabitants." [6]

Another scientist who addresses the issue of absolute unity of existence is David Bohm, an American physicist who lived and worked in Britain and was also a colleague of Einstein's. Bohm theorized what he called an "implicate reality" lying beyond the limits of our "explicate" senses. He said this "implicate order" includes all particles, all electrons, including ourselves and the rest of the universe. While our limited senses see "things", with autonomous, separate existences, Bohm argues for a general law in which all objects and all times are folded together, a law where "everything implicates everything", in an order of undivided wholeness.[7] This is a very different perception, a new paradigm which contradicts the ordinarily held conceptions of reality and of religion.

Existing cultural, geographical, economic and political matters have colored people's perception of God. But, people's perceptions are not and cannot be

---

[6] Paul Davies, *Other Worlds*. New York: Simon and Schuster, 1980, pp.12-3.
[7] David Bohm, *Wholeness and the Implicate Order*. London: Routledge & Kegan Paul, 1982.

the foundation of religion given by God. For example, the common perception is that God existed before people. What is this assumption based on, other than what people imagine? As I mentioned earlier, in mathematics the key to any further research is dependent on acceptance of the preliminary law. Institutionalized religion is not religion. Jesus told a group of people that the donkey remains a donkey, even if you place the Torah on its back. People have been exploited in the name of religion as long as formalized religion has existed. Institutionalized religion, with its nuances of cultural, geographic, economic and political influences, must not be confused with the reality of religion.

"Culture" means the behavior adopted by people and communities in direct response to their natural habitat and surroundings. Geographic location is the placement of the land with respect to the magnetic and gravitational changes on Earth. Politics is the presentation of some people's thoughts, needs, desires and self-interest, vis-à-vis those of others. Economics is the balance between our finite natural environment and the individual's infinite needs and desires. Laws are meant to mediate between natural resources and the instruments used to maintain a balance of power among various political systems. They also protect the self-interest of individuals, groups, nation-states or regional alliances.

The reality of religion transcends these concepts. The most profound mystical experience begins with knowing God and ends with the total absorption and annihilation of the self in God, where nothing but God exists. Each Prophet voiced the experience of the discovered mystery---God. However, the experience was translated by people's imagination and existing religions, cultural and social factors, thereby giving different shapes, forms, attributes and characteristics to an experience that is unbounded and unquantifiable.

For example, in Buddhism, where the concept of God is totally alien to the culture, the transcendent experience of the Buddha (which is timeless and is a result of self-mastery and meditation) is called "Nirvana", whereas in the Abrahamic religious traditions it is called "paradise" or "heaven". The point of divergence in all religious traditions takes place when the experience is formulated into words and images in the minds of those who have not had the experience themselves. The point of convergence is the experience of the one Reality. In the Holy Qur'an (21:92) it is written, "Verily, this Brotherhood of yours is a single Brotherhood, and I am your Lord and Cherisher: therefore worship Me." Only the Reality within us can guide us to the Reality; only when the transient becomes the Reality can one say, "I am the Reality." The expression of union or oneness expressed in the proclamation of faith in Islam is, "la-ilaha-il'Allah"-- "There is no other God but God." It is through submission that the state of oneness is attained. This means that the will of the individual is dissolved in the will of the Absolute, whereby the boundaries of individuation and limitation are demolished. This is the state of total freedom and love which has been amplified in the writings of the Sufi masters.

Physicist David Bohm's general law, described earlier, states that "everything implicates everything." There is no existence but existence. There is no reality but reality. This is the first law of Islam: *La-ilaha-il'Allah.*

Neuroligist Karl Pribram suggests that some people may have discovered a way to cognize Bohm's "implicate order" lying beyond the limits of our "explicate" senses. This feat, he says, would involve learning ways to "abrogate" or get beyond our brain's retrieval systems and micro-electrical codes. Admitting no such experiences himself, Pribram instead refers to the writings of the great mystics of history. Their writings suggest to him that some may have discovered techniques for getting around or beyond the "explicate order" to behold the true nature of reality. He is suggesting that submission to Bohm's general law is how the state of oneness might be attained.[8] This is precisely Sufism's point.

Mansur al-Hallaj, the renowned Sufi of the ninth century, was condemned to death and executed because he said, "I am the Truth." His proclamation of faith is the essence of the teachings of Islam, and to this day it is still misunderstood by Muslim theologians.

---

[8] Karl Pribram interviews in *Psychology Today*, February, 1979, pp.71-84 and *Omni*, October, 1982, pp.129-176

15

The first night, when he was put in prison, the jailers came to see him, but could not find him, and the same thing happened on the second night. On the third night, when they found him, they asked him where he had been. Hallaj answered, "On the first night, I was in the Presence, therefore I was not here. On the second night, the Presence was here, so that both of us were absent. On the third night, I was sent back that the Law might be preserved." [9]

Hazrat Ibrahim Adham's[10] life is a perfect example of the mystic's journey. He was a king who left his throne, his country and his comforts in search of God. It is recounted in the *Tadhkirat al-Awliya* of Farid al-Din Attar that one evening, at midnight, when he was resting on his couch, he heard sounds on the roof of his palace. When he asked who was there and what he was doing there, a voice responded that he was looking for his camel. Adham said, "Fool, do you look for the camel on the roof of my palace?" "Heedless one," answered the voice, "do you seek for God in

---

[9] Farid al-Din Attar, *Muslim Saints and Mystics,* transl. A.J. Arberry. London: Routledge & Kegan Paul Ltd. 1983, p.267.
[10] The fourth Sufi Master in the Maktab Tarighe Oveyssi.

silken clothes, asleep on a golden couch?"[11]   Two
other episodes occurred, each bringing an awakening
to Adham's heart until he finally realized that it was to
God that he must turn.   Through hardship, sacrifice
and self-discipline he tamed the self.   But not until
attaining "union" did he experience the state of
oneness--the release of self and the emergence of the
All.   Each moment of his spiritual journey was one of
death and birth.   From the moment he set out to
discover the answers, to the moment he attained union
with God, each stage reflected various levels of
spiritual purification that he underwent.   Each release
marked a death and a birth, until he experienced the
highest stage, the ultimate release of the self, where
the transient self ceased to exist.

To know what a Sufi speaks about, one must
experience the same.   Then, perhaps the various
stages leading to the proclamation of faith that "there is
no other god but God" will be meaningful.   Otherwise,
words such as "God," "angel," "heaven," "hell," etc.
remain only words that depend on the imagination to
give them shape and form.

---

[11] Attar, *Muslim Saints and Mystics*, p.63.

Sufism teaches that true communication about any experience, mystical or otherwise, must be based on shared inner experiences that are grounded in accurate cognition of our situation. The founder of American psychology and philosophical pragmatism, William James, hinted at this when he wrote that "our experiences are a function of what it is we agree to pay attention to."[12]   To this the Sufis would add "...and, with what faculties we attend, and how."

Sufism instructs humanity that "things are not as they seem," because we pay attention only to the surface of things with our senses and scattered energy. In trying to understand what my words mean, do not confuse words with the experiences giving birth to them. Exchanging words is not the same as exchanging experiences. If you have never seen a sunrise, no words or picture--however scientific, artistic, poetic, etc.--tells you what it is or how it appears. Make comparisons, analogies or metaphors forever, but to know a sunrise, you simply must behold one yourself. A key aphorism of the Oveyssi School is:

---

[12] James, William, *The Principles of Psychology (2 Volumes)*. New York: Holt, Rhineholt, and Winston, 1980. Unaltered republication, New York, Dover, 1950, Volume 1, p. 402.

"words do not convey the meaning." Words, without the validating experiences behind them, are at the heart of all dogma, excesses and misunderstandings plaguing humanity down through the ages.

Socrates, almost two and a half thousand years ago, in his famous *Allegory of the Cave*, [13] describes the perplexity of humanity's situation and state of "unfinished education." He says, shackled head and foot from birth to the cold wall of your cave, you sit mesmerized by the shadows cast by a bonfire out of your direct sight. In your ignorance, you mistake the shadows of real people and objects, parading unseen behind you, for reality itself. Only after someone comes to deliver you miraculously from your chains, are you able to turn around, in pain and protestation, to behold your sad, deluded situation. Only then do you begin to see accurately the reality of events taking place in the cave. With further guidance, you ascend outside to behold the green grass, blue sky, fresh air and, finally, the brilliant sun itself. Completing your education thus requires a teacher.

---

[13] Grube, G.M.A., trans. *The Republic of Plato*. Indianapolis: Hackett, 1974, pp. 170-1.

Socrates discovered, from his own experiences, that he was a prisoner of his senses. This ancient allegory, often treated as some abstract philosophical koan, suddenly becomes enormously relevant when one understands that one lives out one's very life in just such a cave---the one atop the torso: the brain.

This three plus pounds of protoplasm is the source and repository of all one's sensory perceptions, memories, emotions, learning---in short, all of human "psychology" ultimately resides somewhere in the brain's biochemical, electrical mini codes. And, however differently you may sense reality, you live out your entire life in a world of cortical shadows, out of which you construct a limited and totally distorted reality of what "is." In the most literal sense, you are a Cave Dweller.

Modern scientific research, across many disciplines, now validates Socrates' metaphor. We know, for instance, from the sensory sciences, that the eyes see only a tiny fraction of the vast energy that engulfs us. We see "through a glass darkly"---only that sliver of the electromagnetic energy we call the "visible" spectrum. Aldous Huxley equated humanity's situation with that of the frog's, whose visual system only allows it to "see" movement. Whatever is stationary ceases to "exist" for the frog.[14]

Psychologist Robert Ornstein points out that nature is a "cold, quiet, colorless affair outside us." The temperature, colors, and sounds we experience are dimensions of the human experience and not of the world itself, Ornstein reminds us.[15]

In his book on human memory, science writer Philip Hilts made several observation about humanity's cave and the misapprehensions and misperceptions it creates. He presents several key principles in Sufism in a way seldom found in scientific writing. He states that in everyday life, we act as if we have a clear and complete depiction of the world outside us. On the basis of our limited sensory experiences, we imagine wholeness, and think we sense our entire world. There is an enormous disparity between this ordinary experience and what we now know must exist. Our physical senses are capable only of distinguishing a

---

[14] Aldous Huxley, *The Human Situation*. Great Britain: Triad Granada, 1980, p.172.

[15] Robert Ornstein quote from Philip Hilts, *Memory Ghost: The Strange Tale of Mr. M and the Nature of Memory*, New York: Simon and Schuster, 1995, p.222.

minute portion of the electromagnetic spectrum, for example. Despite the new paradigms for science being postulated early in this century, we are just now beginning to understand them, and neither philosophy nor the social sciences have explored the possible consequences. Hilts postulates that, since it usually takes decades, perhaps even centuries, for a radically different vision to be accepted and established, so it must be for this new understanding we are approaching.

> It will require the adoption of a new perspective on life and society, as we are able to absorb it more fully. For the present, we know enough facts to recognize that some of the ways we act and some of the rules of our institutions, which are based on misapprehensions of how minds work, are erroneous. They are misperceptions analogous to optical illusions in the way we view behavior...*[16]*

Scientists in other disciplines have also concluded that humanity's knowledge of reality remains shrouded and incomplete as the frog's, causing our species to suffer its own misperceptions and

---

[16] Philip Hilts, *Memory's Ghost: The Strange Tale of Mr. M and the Nature of Memory.* New York: Simon and Schuster, 1995, p.122.

misapprehensions. For instance, quantum physics also states that humanity does not know reality. In fact, it says, we cannot even imagine it. Evoking Socrates' imagery, Einstein's colleague, Sir Arthur Eddington, once described humanity's situation as "watching a shadowgraph performance of familiar life."[17]

While we tend to believe that science provides a picture of objective reality---of "the world out there", quantum physics has forever crumbled that comfortable sense of reality. What has replaced it is a view of reality so unimaginably bizarre that humanity has yet to face its consequences, just as Hilts' quote suggests from the sensory sciences.

Sufism insists on "first things first" and teaches that humanity has no greater priority than cognizing correctly what is before it, because as just illustrated, science admits it does not know "reality." In fact, science is also beginning to admit its basic ignorance in other critical areas. The late Cornell astronomer

---

[17] Sir Arthur Eddington, *The Nature of the Physical World.* New York: MacMillan, 1929. Quoted from Ken Weber's book, *Quantum Questions: Mystical Writings of the World's Greatest Physicists.* Boulder, CO: Shambhala, 1984, p.9.

Carl Sagan, in a popular scientific journal devoted to "Life in the Universe", raises a stunning definitional problem. Science does not know what "life" is! Sagan says we know that life is more than the usual functions (e.g. ingesting, metabolizing, reproducing, etc.) or matter (nucleic acids, proteins, etc.). But what that something else is, science does not know. In the same issue, Harvard biologist Stephan Jay Gould writes that science does not know why "vertebrates rather than persistent algal mats exist as the most complex forms of life on the earth."[18]

Thus, both modern physics and biology state that humanity remains shrouded from the true reality of existence, believing that it is only what we see, hear, touch, taste and smell that exists. Things are not as they seem!

Neuroscientist Karl Pribram and quantum physicist David Bohm, mentioned earlier, have proposed a model to help explain human consciousness. Their model provides insight into why

---

[18] Special issue of *Scientific American*, entitled *"Life in the Universe."* October 1994. Includes articles by Carl Sagan (*The Search for Extraterrestrial Life*) and Stephen Jay Gould (*The Evolution of Life on the Earth*). Quotes from p.94 and p.86 respectively.

humanity has such problems grasping with its senses and brain the truth of its situation. Their writings intuit some key Sufi principles. For this reason, I want to explore in more detail their writing here.

Their model involves holography, the specialized photography made possible by laser technology. A holograph film is produced when laser light is bounced off some object of interest, creating interference wave patterns. This process produces an interesting result. To the naked eye, a holographically exposed film captures no visible "image" as we know it. However, a laser light used to project the exposed film (much as a slide projector does) "reproduces" the object in a dramatic three-dimensional effect. What is captured holographically on the film simply beggars our very notion of what constitutes reality.

Film exposed to ordinary scattered light produces an instantly recognizable "object", a miniature (albeit a "negative") of what we see with our own eyes. In a holographic film, "objects" appear literally nowhere, yet are everywhere in the film. Such film can be cut into many pieces, yet the entire "object" of interest remains in every piece. The holograph presents a different reality from that provided by a lens-defined or "objective" model of the world ("objective," as in the lens of a microscope, telescope or human eye).

Karl Pribram is interested in the holograph as a model, or metaphor, to help explain certain brain functions, including such mysteries as memory loss (our memory, for instance, seems to be distributed throughout the brain and located nowhere specifically), the maintenance of "constancy" (recognizing an object, regardless of its distance or orientation with respect to the viewer), and the transfer of skills from one limb of our body to another.

David Bohm, the quantum physicist, uses the hologram as a model to illustrate the existence of an "implicate reality" lying beyond the limits of our "explicate" senses. He offers the difference between the common photographic "negative" and the hologram as an analogy, respectively, of his "explicate" and "implicate" orders of reality. He describes a new concept of "reality" for the theoretical physicist and sensory scientist to consider. As indicated earlier, he makes it clear that we must cease to consider the particles, which physics had previously considered the basic constituents of matter, to be independent and separate. The term "electron" should be viewed as no more than a name, a label which we use to call attention to a certain demonstrated phenomenon. It is an aspect which can be accurately discussed only in terms of the entire experimental context, and that cannot be specific in terms of an individual, material object moving independently in a specific location.

> Thus, we come to a new general physical description in which 'everything implicates everything' in an order of undivided wholeness...'All implicates all', even to the extent that 'we ourselves' are implicated together with 'all that we see and think about.' So, we are present everywhere and at all times, though only implicately (that is implicitly). The same is true of every 'object.'[19]

Karl Pribram suggests that scientific sense can now be made out of the mystical experiences which people have been describing for millennia. Although what he states is not a part of his own experience, he cannot help but wonder if somehow the mystics have not discovered a mechanism which permits them to tap into the order of reality that is behind the world of

---

[19] Bohm, David. *op cit.* p. 167.

appearances, to tap into the implicate order. He believes that to do so would "be a matter of abrogating our retrieval systems so that we can experience the brain's minicodes." [20] We would ignore our senses, our "lenses" and experience only the frequency domain.

> The purpose of science is to make sense of the world, and mystical experience makes sense when one can provide the mathematical transform that one takes back and forth between the ordinary image-object domain and the frequency domain. [21]

Pribram is in agreement with the most basic teachings of the Sufis when he suggests that the mystics may have discovered a way to cognize Bohm's implicate order, by learning ways to "abrogate," or get around, our brain's retrieval systems and micro-electrical codes.

In the best scientific tradition of open skepticism, admitting no personal knowledge replicating such experiences for himself, Pribram instead refers interested parties to the writings of the great mystics of history. Their writings suggest to him that some have

---

[20] Karl Pribram interview in *Omni*, October, 1982, p.172.
[21] Pribram, ibid, p. 172.

discovered techniques to getting around or beyond the "explicate order," to behold the true nature of our reality as human beings.

By introducing their new view of the world, Pribram and Bohm challenge science's most cherished concepts of reality, of causality, of time and space, and the very language we must rely on to describe the world to ourselves and others. Pribram, in discussing the concepts underlying the holographic process, writes the following:

> It is mind boggling. The frequency domain deals with the density of occurrences only; time and space are collapsed. Ordinary boundaries of space and time, such as locations of any sort, disappear... In the absence of space-time coordinates, the causality upon which most scientific explanations depend is also suspended.[22]

Our communication methods create immense communication barriers for understanding this different view of "reality." The very structure of language, the necessity to include subject-verb-object, regardless of the order, is a world view, and it imposes itself strongly when we speak, even in cases which seem evidently

---

[22] Pribram, Karl. *op. cit.*, 1979, p. 84.

inappropriate. As an example, Bohm asks where is the "It", that would, according to the sentence "It is raining", be the "rainer" that is doing the raining? In a similar manner, Bohm continues, we usually state that one elementary particle acts on another, yet each "particle" is only "...an abstraction of a relatively invariant form of movement in the whole field of the universe." It would actually be more accurate to say that "...elementary particles are on-going movements that are mutually dependent because ultimately they merge and interpenetrate." The same sort of description is also more appropriate on a larger scale. Instead of stating that an observer looks at an object, it is more appropriate to say that observation is occurring, in an undivided moment involving the abstractions we usually call "the human being" and "the object he is looking at." [23]

The benefits from this new view of reality and the order of the universe have unparalleled implications for humanity. For instance, Pribram states: "For the first time in three hundred years, science is admitting spiritual values into its

---

[23] David Bohm, *op. cit.*, p.29

explorations. That's terribly important." [24] Bohm states that the ground of all that is is "...enfolded in our consciousness..." Although we have no detailed perception or knowledge of this ground, nevertheless, it is an integral part of our being. He sees the very nature of the universe, of matter, of life and of consciousness as projections of a common ground. [25]

Because humanity fails to perceive or cognize its true situation in existence, just as Socrates describes in his Cave Analogy, it also fails to understand the true meaning of religion, which is to know the truth of existence. To understand the reality of religion is to know the truth of your constant Self and God. It is your very neural equipment which gives shape and form to the little god you create in your mind, which separates you from God, the reality of your Self, the reality of your existence.

Amir al-Mo'menin Ali (peace be upon him), the revered Lord of the Sufis and the first Imam of the Shi'a, has said, "I am astounded at people who do not know their own self and want to know God." Generally,

---

[24] Karl Pribram, *op.cit.*, 1982, p.174
[25] David Bohm, *op.cit.*, p.212-3.

people think that they know God. They assume that there is a God who created us and then left us to ourselves. That is, He left us to our own limitations to continue the process of creation that He set in motion at some unknown time. When the day of Judgment comes, we assume He will appear again to determine our fate and that He will then either send us to heaven or hell.

People think that hell is a place where there is fire and torment and that those who have been evil will burn in the fire. Heaven is visualized as a splendid garden, where one's dreams and wishes will be realized. Each person lives in the hell or heaven that he or she has created and will continue to do so after this life. People assume that they will be traveling somewhere after they die. The Prophet Muhammad (peace be upon him) said, "Whichever way you live here, that's how you will continue thereafter." If you are disturbed and anxious in this life, that's how you will continue to be. This is the hell in which you will be, here and thereafter. The disquiet, the anger, the greed, the jealousy that people live with, that is their hell and that is how they will continue after their earthly life. Life on earth is a minuscule, and yet very important, part of the infinite life of each human being. It is minuscule when compared to the infinite, and it is important because all the tools needed for becoming infinite and eternal are provided in the human form.

If you look at death simply as a process of leaving one room and entering another, you will begin to understand the misconceptions associated with it. When you leave one room and enter another, you still take with you your knowledge, likes, dislikes, hatreds, anger and all the other attributes that you have, as well as your wealth, family and all other possessions. None of these cease because you have entered another room. Death does not mean that you cease to exist. All that ceases to exist is your current molecular form which slowly starts to change, disintegrate and integrate with nature again. The "I" behind the physical form, that entity we refer to as the "self", will continue to exist when the body ceases to function as a unit.

When one discovers God, one finds heaven on earth. It is by knowing God that a life based on continuous changes and uncertainties is transformed into a life founded upon firm knowledge and stability.

Conventional thinking says that God is somewhere and we are here, and to Him we shall return. Is such a God absolute? How can God be absolute, if He is not everywhere? There is the place that He is not? And what is in that place and what is it like? Mathematically and scientifically it is impossible to prove that He is somewhere and not elsewhere. The problem exists because people have given a shape and form to God in their minds and have separated themselves from God. It was the Prophet Abraham who shattered all the idols in the temple to tell people that the idols they had created with their own hands could not be the Creator who is Absolute. In essence, he was telling people not to worship a god who was the product of their imagination, because such a god is limited and not worthy of worship. When God is cognized inwardly, one knows that God is Ever-present and Absolute. There is an interesting lesson taught by a Sufi master who told one of his students to take a chicken and kill it out of God's sight. The student returned a few days later with the chicken alive in his hand. The master asked him why he had not killed the chicken. The student said that he could not find a place where God was not.

The essential message of the Prophets, as stated in the words of the Prophet Muhammad (peace be upon him), is, "Die before you die." This means die from your human self, lift the veil that covers your reality so that you may live in peace here and forever. The teachings of Islam, as taught by the Prophet Muhammad and kept alive by those whom he confirmed, are for this purpose--to teach how to arrive at one's reality, the divinity within. This process is called purification.

The serious seeker distinguishes between experiential religion and institutionalized religion, and is bent on discovering the inner experience of religion. To attain the state of knowing, both must be present. If you look at the lives of the Prophets, you will see that they led a very disciplined life. Their efforts were directed toward self-purification, service and devotion to God. They relinquished whatever came between them and God. The spiritual life has its own rules, which must be observed with perseverance, devotion and love. Just as one cannot become a great scientist, musician, artist or athlete without effort, practice and commitment, attaining spiritual elevation cannot be realized without fulfilling its requirements.

If you look at the five prescribed daily prayers in Islam, you will see their significance. If observed as they should be, that is, with nothing standing between the praying person and God, their results will be seen in one's daily life. The Holy Prophet Muhammad (peace and blessings upon him) has said, "The pure believer in his devotion to God is like clear, pure water, as when it falls from the sky."[26]

How can someone pray in earnest five times a day with a yearning heart and mind for God, witness God, submit his total self to the will of God, and not have God's love in his heart? How can such a person act with disrespect and hatred? How can such a person ever abuse anyone or anything? How can such a person be intolerant? Any act of devotion, if observed blindly, will not bring the needed results. The human being has two aspects, one that is continuously drawn to the earth, and another that aspires to ascend

---

[26] Molana Shah Maghsoud Sadegh Angha, *Al Rasa'el*. Lanham: University Press of America, 1986, p.42.

to the heavens. Religion, in its true sense, is a means of transforming the earthly human being into his or her heavenly self. The daily prayers in Islam are a constant reminder for believers, to keep them on the path of true human dignity as ordained by God. The prayers are a source of strength for the true believer, whose only goal is closeness to God.

Rising (*qiyam*) for prayer means rising from one's stable foundation and not leaning towards anything. The first step in prayer is to rise and to stand firm, with the intention of witnessing God and attesting to the oneness of God.

Let me provide an example. Consider a date tree. When the date tree is growing, its roots move into the earth, searching for the very source of water. Even if the roots encounter a puddle of water while searching on their path of discovery, they do not get diverted, they keep moving until they find the source of water. As soon as they reach the source, the leaves, which had been yellow up to that time, become green and healthy-looking. After a short time, the tree gives its first dates. However, it takes 90 years before the tree produces its finest dates. This shows the tree's innate submission to its own point of origin, as well as its patience and endurance until the final result is obtained.

Islam means submission, but not to an unknown god. Rather, it is based on certainty, which is the result of seeing and knowing. Submitting to a god of our imagination is just as fatal as submitting to a dictator and is the best way for innocent and ignorant minds to be manipulated in the name of religion. The reality of submission is seen in the bloom of the rose, in the apple tree bearing healthy apples, in the brilliance of the moon. Each one manifests one law: submission to knowledge. It is knowledge that is capable of manifesting the rose, the tree, and all else in their completeness.

Unfortunately, human beings usually are not in harmony with themselves, but behave according to their inclinations, which are a response to external activities. They expend their energy in this manner. Because they do not persist to the end of their search, they do not reap the necessary reward from their effort.

What is of concern to us here is attaining a state of harmony with our self, which, in essence, means oneness with Existence. Its prerequisite is an innate likeness. For example, when you place a stone next to a fire, the stone gradually absorbs heat from the fire. If you touch the stone after a while, you will see that it has become warm, but that is the extent of it. Why? Because the stone does not have the same innate quality as the fire. If you increase the heat, and place the stone in the fire, it will eventually shatter into pieces. The stone is capable of absorbing heat to a certain point, but no more. If you increase the heat substantially from the beginning, the stone will shatter even more quickly. Why? Because the stone is hard and dense and its properties are different from those of the fire.

In contrast, if you place a piece of charcoal next to the fire, you will see that it gradually absorbs the heat and becomes hot and red. It puts forth the heat from inside itself. That is to say, it becomes a manifestation of the fire and shows it. Why? Because it has the capacity of acceptance. Because it is of the same quality as fire and in harmony with it. This means that the quality of the fire is with the charcoal. When it is placed next to the fire, it manifests the same heat and redness. And, when it eventually burns out, it does not shatter to pieces, but rather, gradually, and as a unit, turns to ash. This process represents submission, annihilation, knowledge and unification.

The important point to recognize here is that, to discover the Truth, one must be in harmony and have the capacity to accept. If this principle does not exist, any encounter will only be superficial, like the relationship of the stone and the fire. Whereas the charcoal, through its encounter and proximity with the fire, presented the fire that it inherently had the capacity to be. The capacity of acceptance and harmony was what brought forth that innate capacity of the charcoal, which was fire. One piece of red hot charcoal sets the charcoals surrounding it on fire as well.

If you expand this example, you will see that is also holds true for human beings. People generally take on the colors of their surroundings. Although human beings are created in the image of God and are supposed to be the chosen of Creation, they are unable to manifest that innate essence. Instead, people are continuously influenced by their surroundings and unable to attain a state of stability, well-being and peace.

The Prophets exemplify the reality of submission, which made them able to receive revelation. If we put aside all the theological disputes concerning revelation, we see it to be a form of divinely revealed, disclosed information.

In general, when we speak of darkness, we mean a situation in which there is no light and, therefore, nothing can be seen or known. However, I must point out that in such a situation, light particles nonetheless exist, although we cannot see them, and we call it darkness. Whereas, whatever was unknown in the dark is revealed when things are brought into the light. We usually say that, wherever knowledge exists, the darkness of ignorance is expelled. The most significant aspect of revelation is that it gives knowledge of the unknown. It brings certainty and replaces blind faith. It illuminates what was hidden.

The holy scriptures of any faith must be read with the light of revelation. To know the word of God, one must be in harmony with it. The discovery of the meaning depends on the receptivity of the reader.

Being receptive means having one's receptors activated and in harmony. For example, after a child is born, the more his mother caresses and cuddles him, the more his receptors are activated. This process enhances the child's receptivity on a physical and emotional level. We also see a similar process in animals such as dogs, cats, sheep and cows. The mother licks the newborn. This process activates the receptors in the newborn. In other words, on the physical level it is necessary for the receptors to become activated so that the offspring's survival can be enhanced. Developmental research has established the critical importance of close tactile simulation with human infants. As reported in most introductory developmental psychology texts, to deprive a child of it can mean severe physical and mental dysfunction, even death.

Just as it is necessary for our receptors to be developed on a physical level, it is equally important that we develop the receptors that involve our spiritual evolution, so that our capacity for the reception of divine matters can be attained.

Sufism says that before we humans can truly communicate, find peace, understand nature, promote human rights or have an accurate psychology, we must come to discover a hidden dimension within ourselves. This faculty, this receptor, enables us to cognize accurately our true situation, as Pribram speculated when he wrote about "abrogating our retrieval system."

On any level of human interaction, harmony is necessary if communication is to be established. It takes harmony between the listener and speaker so that communication may take place. The fewer mental distractions the listener has, the more focused he is, the more he is capable of understanding what the speaker is saying. The same is required to discover the spiritual depth and subtleties of the words of God, which are received through revelation.

When the urge for discovery is vital to a person, the answer accompanies it. By this, I mean that the receptivity to learn, develop and discover is present. There is an innate harmony between the speaker and the listener. This holds true in any learning situation, including scientific experimentation. Here I am speaking of a discovery that encompasses all discovery--the Absolute Reality.

What does revelation entail? How does it happen? Is it a gift endowed to a few? If not, how can one be in a position to receive revelation? It must be remembered that the limited cannot define the unlimited. That is to say, the human being who has not broken the boundaries of limitation cannot define the Absolute. Existence is infinite. Existence exists, therefore a being called the human exists. There is nothing void of Existence.

The tools useful in the limited world cannot resolve the questions concerning the unlimited. For example, you say that you want to know God. And I say, in order to know God, you must see and hear God. But how? You say that you cannot. Why?

It is true that you have the ability to hear, but your hearing, limited to picking up only certain sound frequencies and amplitudes, is not using its maximum capacity. For example, the reason you can hear my voice right now is the microphone. If this microphone were turned off, and the sound wave frequency and amplitude of my voice did not interact with your

44

eardrums, you would not be able to hear me. What we call hearing is nothing more than the interaction of certain characteristics of sound waves with the hearing mechanism involving our outer, middle and inner ears, and ultimately, our auditory cortex. However, true hearing exists in its absolute form and is not dependent on the physical characteristics of sound energy. As long as hearing is limited to the frequency and amplitude of sound waves, "cognition" and "revelation" are not possible. In order for you to hear me, you must be in harmony with the same energy as I am. And, to be in harmony with the same energy requires that you be made of the same spirit as I am. When you and I are of the same spirit, it is then that we are of the same energy and, whatever I say, you will hear and understand.

This is the meaning of what God has said, "Say: I am a human being like you, but I receive revelation." (Holy Qur'an, 18:110) Because the Holy Prophet is of the exact same spirit as God, whatever God says, he hears the same. You say that you want to hear God. You must know and become one with God and be of the same spirit as God.

The same concept holds true for seeing. You have the necessary tools for seeing, that is, you have eyes, but because you use them only for the refraction of light, they only see the surface of things. You do not cognize the quality of sight at its absolute level.

Surface scientists working with electron microscopes tend to agree with those ancients who claimed that "the devil dwells on the surface of things."

As previously noted, both modern physics and biology state that humanity remains shrouded from the true reality of existence, believing only that it is what we see, hear, touch, taste and smell that exists. Things indeed are not as they seem! We must learn a radically new way of seeing, for humanity's education is incomplete.

The Holy Prophet Jesus, who often commanded that "let he who has ears hear, and he who has eyes see," also said: "I shall give you what no eye has seen and what no ear has heard and what no hand has touched and what has never occurred to the human mind." [27]

---

[27] James M. Robinson, ed., *The Nag Hammadi Library* (Translated by members of the Coptic Gnostic Library Project of the Institute for

Sight is independent of muscles, eyelashes, nerves, and lenses. That is to say, sight is not bound by physiological mechanisms and, hence, does not limit itself to the eyes. Sight is infinite and absolute, although its manifestation is through the visual mechanisms named above. Having eyes does not affect seeing. Vision is innately present in the human being, but since it is only directed to the surface of things, that is all that the eyes see. For example, if your eyes are in optimum condition, but there is no light, you will not be able to see. Even when you turn on the light, your eyes take some time to adjust to the changed condition. But true sight is not bound to any such external conditions.

Sufism completes humanity's education. It answers ultimate questions about who you are, where you come from, and where you are going. It unchains you from your cave and allows you to cognize the reality underlying all of existence and to learn how to use wisely the riches already bestowed on you by existence. A Sufi analogy says the banquet is already

Antiquity and Christianity). New York: Harper and Row, 1977, pp120, 17.

47

before humanity, but we simply do not experience it because we are looking the wrong way.

Whatever Existence has, you also have. All that exists is imbued with Existence, nothing is apart from Existence. To attain the state of "hearing" and "seeing," you must be elevated from the lowest state of your existence, which is your physical level, to your most elevated state, which is called "*adamiyyat*"[28]---the chosen of Creation--as created in the image of God.

There are many verses in the Holy Qur'an which speak of the various ways that God reveals Himself to His creation. These are called *ayat* (signs). Hence, the *ayat* (verses) of the Holy Qur'an speak to those whose hearts have been illuminated by the light of Knowledge. The Holy Qur'an (42: 51-53) states,

> *It is not fitting for a man that God should speak to him except by inspiration, or from behind a veil, or by the sending of a Messenger to reveal, with God's permission, what God wills: for He is Most High, Most Wise. And thus have We, by Our command, sent Inspiration to thee: Thou knewest not (before) what was Revelation, and what was*

---

[28] Persian adjective, based on the Arabic proper name, Adam, literally "pertaining to Adam," with the common meaning "humanity." In Persian mystical literature the term signifies the quintessential positive attribute of the concept "humanity," or "humanness."

*Faith; but We have made the (Qur-an) a Light, wherewith
We guide such of Our servants as We will; and verily thou
dost guide (men) to the Straight Way.*

The Holy Prophet Muhammad (peace and
blessings upon him) has said, "Knowledge is not
obtained through scholarship but it is a light that God
shines in the heart of whomever He desires."

Throughout time, God has revealed Himself in a
unique manner to each of His Prophets. The following
are a few examples as cited in the Holy Qur'an:

*(Remember) Noah, when he cried (to Us) aforetime: We
listened to his (prayer) and delivered him and his family
from great distress. (21:76)*

*To Solomon We inspired the (right) understanding of the
matter: to each We gave Judgment and Knowledge.
(21:79)*

*We bestowed aforetime on Abraham his rectitude of
conduct, and well were We acquainted with him. (21:51)*

*In the past We granted to Moses and Aaron the Criterion
(for judgment), and a Light and a Message for those who
would do right. (21:48)*

And (remember) Zakariya, when he cried to his Lord: "O my Lord! Leave me not without offspring, Thou art the best of inheritors." (21:89)

So We listened to him: and We granted him Yahya: We cured his wife's (barrenness) for him. (21:90)

And (remember) her who guarded her chastity: We breathed into her of Our Spirit, and We made her and her son a Sign for all peoples. (21:91)

It is said that there are 99 names of Allah mentioned in the Holy Qur'an. Each name is indicative of a unique discovery, and shows that a communication had been established and a revelation had taken place. Should we not ask why 99 names and not 100? The 99 names reflect the attributes of the One. The discovery of the One must have been the starting point, so that the 99 names could follow. This results in 100 and, according to the science of letters and numbers, returns to its origin, thereby becoming One. If the One was not discovered, how could the names have come into being? Whom would they be describing? The subject must always be present before any attributes can be ascribed to it.

The following verses from the Holy Qur'an speak about seeking the Face or the Countenance of God, and, yet, it is considered sacrilege by Muslim clerics and jurists to say that God must be seen before certainty in faith can be established:

Withersoever you turn, there is the Face of God. (2:115)
Patient men, desirous of the Face of their Lord. (13:22)
All things perish, except His Face. (18:28)
That is better for those who desire God's Face. (30:38)
Abides the Face of thy Lord, majestic, splendid. (55:27)
Only seeking the Face of his Lord the Most High. (92:20)

Islam is founded upon submission, but how can one submit to an unknown? Blind faith is a result of submitting to an unknown god formulated in people's imagination. It is not the God of whom the Prophets have spoken. In Sura Baqara of the Holy Qur'an (2:2-3), it is stated that it is a Book for those "who believe in the Unseen." The "Unseen" has been taken to mean that it is beyond human capacity to know God, therefore one must accept blindly or on "faith." How much certainty is there in a faith whose only foundation is what someone else has told you? Mola Amir al-Mo'menin, the Imam Ali, has said, "Faith is manifested in the heart as a ray of light, and as faith increases, the light spreads."[29]

Faith must be based on certainty which comes from direct cognition or knowing. It is recorded that: "The devout Za'lab Yamani asked Amir al-Mo'menin Ali (peace be upon him): 'Have you seen God?' He replied: 'Would I worship a God whom I have not seen?' Yamani then asked: 'How have you seen Him?' He said: 'He is not visible to the eye, whereas the heart beholds Him with the reality of faith. However, seeing is witnessing of the eye and at times it is applied to the inner faculties and the heart. But absolute vision is when knowledge is unveiled to the heart at three levels, the elevated wisdom, the moderate wisdom, and the inferior wisdom.'"[30]

The human system has a built-in mechanism capable of receiving revelation. According to the teachings of the Oveyssi Shahmaghsoudi School of Sufism, the human body is equipped with 13 electromagnetic centers whose function is vital to the

[29] *Al-Rasa'el*, p.38.
[30] *Al-Rasa'el*, p.38-39.

well-being of individuals, as well as their metaphysical and spiritual life.

The most important of these centers resides in the heart. The cardiovascular system is the first system to function in the embryo. The earliest sign of the heart is the appearance of paired tissue during the third week of gestation. These cords then become tubes, which fuse to form a single chamber. With further development, because the ventricle grows faster than other regions, the cardiac tube bends itself, forming a U-shaped loop.

Contractions of the heart in the sinus venosus begin by the $21^{st}/22^{nd}$ day after conception. The site of our primordial biological pacemaker (that which controls the electrical activity of the heart) is in this primitive atrium. The Sino-atrial node develops during the fifth week of gestation. It is originally located in the right wall of the atrium, but, with further development of the heart, it becomes incorporated into the *Crista Terminalis*, which is the remnant of the sinus venosus, the site of the "primordial pacemaker."

According to the teachings of the Oveyssi Shahmaghsoudi School of Sufism, this *Christa*

Terminalis is the most important energy source of the body. My father, Molana Shah Maghsoud Sadegh Angha, who is the forty-first Master of the School, has referred to it as "the source of life in the heart." This source is the gateway to the human being's spiritual realm, as it is the doorway to the heavenly kingdom of God.

The energy created by this "primordial pacemaker" is closely tied in with the bio-electrical mechanisms of the heart, as mediated by the cardiac plexuses (conglomerates of nerve fibers). The heart is innervated by those neurons in our autonomic nervous system which excite us (the sympathetic nerves) and calm us (the parasympathetic nerves). Our heart's excitation arises from the main trunk of neck and upper thoracic neurons of the right atrium of our heart.

The autonomic nervous system's role in exciting and calming our heart is mediated by our 10th pair of cranial nerves, the vagus nerve. This nerve consists of motor (afferent) neurons which innervate the muscles of the heart, through the nodes described earlier and the complex of neurons around the coronary arteries. The vagus nerve also includes sensory (efferent) neurons which relay messages back to the brain and take part in our cardiovascular reflexes. These afferent fibers, running with the sympathetic nerves, carry nervous impulses from the heart back to the central nervous system. These pathways are directed both to the brain stem and cerebral cortex. We know, for example, that in cases where the blood supply to the myocardium (the muscular substance of the heart) becomes compromised, pain impulses reach consciousness via this pathway.

As previously indicated, the importance of the heart is repeated throughout the Holy Qur'an and Holy Bible. For example, prayer in Islam begins with the Sura al-Fatiha (1:1-7): "In the Name of God, the Compassionate, the Merciful---O God lead us to the Straight Path..." It is by straightening the connection between the heart and the brain that the brain is illuminated.

In Western medicine, it is believed that the brain is the control center of the whole body. However, the heart is the ultimate center that commands the brain, which in turn commands the body. In other words, in the Western tradition the primary relationship is: brain-

→ heart and brain-→ body; whereas the ultimate relationship should be: heart-→ brain-→ body. In this light, the words of the prayer mentioned above take on a new meaning: the path between the heart and the brain becomes "straightened" or reversed.

In 1968, my father in his book entitled *Message from the Soul* wrote:

> There are one hundred and one channels, starting from the source of life in the heart through which seventy one thousand lines irrigate the ten billion brain cells, so that the creation of God in this diffusion and gathering is brought to perfection. The source of life resides on the border between the heavens and the earth, and serves the will of God. At the point where the consciousness of life and the sleep of death confront each other, the first longs for eternity and the latter is attracted towards transience.
>
> Search for truth in your heavenly double, at a third point in the heart, the point of union of the two worlds, one delicate and one harsh, between sleep and wakefulness. The source of life in the heart is the light of knowledge and certainty, and the very knowledge itself. And because it is all-knowing, it is the source of all appearances and possibilities. It is the essence and the body of all things. Everything is brought to perfection by it.[31]

---

[31] Molana Shah Maghsoud Sadegh Angha, "Message from the Soul," reprinted in idem., *The Mystery of Humanity: Survival and Tranquillity*. Lanham: University Press of America, 1996, pp. 63-64.

The "Primordial Knot" is "dormant," for lack of a better term. Through meditation and prayer, it is "awakened" and the pathway between the heart and brain thus becomes "illuminated." A reversal occurs in the relationship between the two entities, in such a way that the "polarity" of the heart gains its due sovereignty over the realm of the brain: this is the fundamental essence of the aforementioned opening verse of the Holy Qur'an.

The electrical properties of the heart have been used in Western medicine through the technology of the electrocardiograph, the EKG. The magnetic properties of the body, in general, and the heart, in particular, even though measurable, have been ignored by medical science because of a lack of understanding of their importance. And, unfortunately, because the electromagnetic centers of the body are not externally visible, their existence, function, and properties remain a mystery.

Revelation, like many other aspects of religion, has remained in obscurity and usually been considered to be beyond the reach of human beings. Islam is a religion of knowledge which has been revealed and entrusted to its keepers through time. As it has been recorded in the Sacred Hadith: "The earth and the skies cannot contain Me, but the heart of My pious and virtuous servant is able to behold Me."[32]

As demonstrated, the human system has a built-in mechanism to receive revelation. It requires readiness and harmony on the part of the recipient. The field of electromagnetic centers and its relationship with the spiritual training received by the student of Sufism is extensive. Each of the 13 main centers has a specific function and is connected to special electromagnetic and universal energy sources. For a better understanding of the energy centers, you can refer to *The Hidden Angles of Life* written by my father, and to my book being prepared for publication entitled *Dam* (or *Breath*), in which I explain in detail these matters.

What is of essence in the teachings of Islam is freedom and well-being, which means that you, as an individual in your own time, must experience the truth of its teaching. Islam is not an act of postponement. When you are well, all else proceeds from that

---

[32] *Al-Rasa'el*, p.13

wellness. When you are not, it means you have been susceptible to changes, resulting from a series of external and volatile actions. What does this mean? It means that health is not with you and you are not grounded in your vital center. Generally, your actions reflect what you are influenced by. This holds true for daily matters, as well as spiritual ones.

Notice that, when looking for a job, to be successful you apply for positions close to what you have studied and know. This same principle of balance and health presents the centrality and point of balance in your being. This principle must be present with human beings so that their actions may be fruitful. Otherwise, you may spend time and energy, work hard, but not obtain the desired results.

The same holds true for spiritual seekers. You may observe your prayers, fast, etc., but still not get the results you wanted. You do not reach the Reality you seek. Why? Because your actions are only a series of external activities having no roots in an inner foundation.

As I mentioned earlier, the self has two aspects. It can either be heavenly or beastly. The beastly self is influenced by external things and events, while the heavenly self is submitted to God. The results of each are evident.

To give you a clearer picture, let me provide this example. Consider a circle with two aspects, that is, with a horizontal and a vertical axis. The vertical axis represents the heavenly realm and your ascent. The horizontal axis represents the earthly realm and your descent. Each is founded upon and rises from a central point. That is to say, they can represent both the ascent and the descent, depending on where the self leads you.

The self is a tender and expansive essence which encompasses all things. If it is attentive to the divine command, its journey is beyond the realm of nature, thereby being eternal and unchangeable. But if it is inclined towards the realm of changes and limitation, its ultimate journey will be the cellular life and the changes that result in it. When death takes place, its journey will be the extent of what it has attained and known. Spinoza, the 17th century philosopher, stated this principle as follows:

The soul has the choice of uniting with the body, whose idea it is, or with God, without whom it cannot subsist or be conceived of. If it is united only with the body, it must die with the body. But, if it unites with something that is immutable and enduring, it will necessarily endure with it.[33]

The famous Swiss psychotherapist Carl Jung, speculated about the "Self," holding that it embraced the center of our totality. Jung went on to speculate about a major principle in Sufism. He said that the great spiritual leaders of humanity, the ones we call Prophets, must be understood as role models to show us how to reach life's ultimate goal ---Self-discovery. Jung said that, "though we know of this Self, yet it is not known," and then concluded that:

if the Self could be wholly experienced, it would be a limited experience, whereas in reality its experience is unlimited and endless...If I were one with the Self, I would have knowledge of everything.[34]

Unfortunately, Jung died without cognizing what he deemed to be the centrality of his existence.

Just as a mine is capable of producing diamonds, it can also be barren---producing only dust.

---

[33] Karl Jaspers, *op.cit.*, pp.42, 61.

[34] Carl Jung, *Letters, Vol II 1951-1961*. (G. Adler, ed.), Princeton, NJ: Princeton University Press, 1975, pp.194-5.

The human being is the same; you can excavate the ultimate treasure which is within you, or you can spend your time and energy on all the short-lived things of the earth, and eventually remain empty-handed. The Holy Prophet Muhammad (peace and blessings upon him) has said: "Each human being is like a mine---gold, silver or jewel---excavate the goodness within them, so that you may have peace." The Holy Prophet Jesus provided instructions on the importance of mining, of bringing forth, that which we have within us: "That which you have will save you, if you bring it forth from yourselves."[35] The energy fields that you are expand and extend to the galaxies. In this human structure, in this form that you are, you have the capacity to ascend to the highest rank as ordained, or, you can be satisfied with whatever you have.

I mentioned ascending to the rank of *adamiyyat* (Adam). The Prophets, Saints and the Chosen are examples of this ascendance. You too must become in harmony and on the same frequency so that you can hear God. For this to take place, it is necessary that you be on the journey of ascent of the Self.

---

[35] James Robinson, *op. cit.*, p. 126.

We have all heard that people become like those with whom they mix. If you associate with a vagabond, you begin behaving and talking like one. If you associate with a wise person, you begin behaving and talking like one. If you observe gamblers closely, you will see that all their actions reflect what is of importance to them. Why? Because they are totally immersed in gambling. Influenced by it, they expand themselves into this world.

Researchers are the same; their focus is simply on something else. They become absorbed in the subject under investigation. Even sleep does not interrupt this process. At times, they may even make certain discoveries in their sleep. Why? Because the researchers become an extension of what they are interested in and all their energies are directed there. It is this focus and concentration that allows them to make their discoveries.

Now, what must you do? First, you must be free and well. Free from what? Free from all the things that attract your attention and energies to themselves and take you away from your point of stability and constancy. How do you become free? Purification.

And, what does this mean? It means to submit and then act. When submission is followed by acts of devotion, the self will be drawn from the earth toward its heavenly realm. When you are emptied of your earthly attributes you will be endowed with your divine attributes. All acts of devotion must be founded upon love and sincerity. Islam is a religion of tolerance and freedom, because it is founded on knowledge and love.

Religion that has not been revealed by God is not religion, but a set of cultural, ethnic and family beliefs that are handed down from one generation to another and that people follow without knowing their true meaning or value. The promulgator of each faith spoke of his own discoveries and laid down certain guidelines for those aspiring to discover the same. They did not say, "Follow me blindly." They had not followed anyone blindly, so how could they ask anyone else to do what they had not done? They shared their wisdom and knowledge, because it was their duty to do so. In the same manner, scientists announce the results of their discoveries for the benefit of humanity. If you ask a believer of each faith about the deity they worship, you will see that it is the image in people's minds that creates the boundaries between each faith. The disputes and misunderstandings between the followers of each faith revolve around an image they have formed around a name they are bent on protecting. If Buddha, Moses, Jesus and Muhammad (peace upon them) were in the same room, would they fight each other or would they understand each other? Would there be a common "knowing" among them, or would they dispute one another? Would their experiences of the ever eternal, Self-Subsisting Existence be one and the same or different?

Wisdom and knowledge cannot be imposed or given to anyone. It takes a sincere aspirant who makes every effort to discover the ultimate gift of Existence--Self-Knowledge. As the Holy Prophet Muhammad (peace be upon him) said, "Whoever knows the true Self, knows God."

The seeker who undergoes the various stages of self-discipline and purification and for whom the veils of the unknowns have been lifted, with faith and knowledge, attests to the Oneness of God. He or she knows that there is no duality nor separation between him or her and Existence, for whatever exists in submission forever glorifies the essence of Existence.

Survival and submission go hand in hand. The instinct to survive, or to "live," is innate in each creature. This is why the date tree roots strive with patience and perseverance until the tree bears its best fruit after 90 years. The fragrance of the rose is the flower's declaration of its liberation from containment to formlessness and expansion. The human being has been given the gift of eternity which is borne of submission to God. Annihilation in God results in eternal existence. The ultimate decision belongs to the human being: How much of your share of existence are you willing to work for?

Life is a gift for those who understand and cognize themselves---for those who know who they are. By "knowing", I do not mean the various cultural, educational, and environmental factors by which you identify yourself. The person who truly knows himself or herself, will be in total harmony with all of existence. The reality of each individual is that which is stable and constant. Each human being is the center of the universe. The center has everything in its own power, like the circle and its center. The center is the cause of the circle, and not vice versa. This center is real and exists in everything.

People think that if they adjust themselves to society, they will have stability. But, how can anything that is forever changing bring stability? One must be in harmony with that which is stable and constant. If you want to know about all of existence, you have to be existence. The essential thing is that you are existence. But you limit yourself to the dependencies of your senses, which only present a very small aspect of existence. Life is absolute and is not limited to the senses. Life is the source of all behavior and all manifestations; therefore it is everlasting. When you are at the center of your being then you will be able to see everything from all angles---from 360 degrees. When you reach this point, you are free and no longer limited to the physical boundaries of your body. This state in Sufism is called annihilation (*fana*) and permanence (*baqa*) in God.

People usually blame God for the injustices of the world. But if you stop and reflect, you will see that it is people who are unjust. The history of humanity bears testimony to the cruelties and injustices of people against one another. People rise up and fight against injustice, because the innate nature of humans is to be free. Yet, we see that each revolution devours its own children. People who have risen against injustice, in turn become the dictators of their societies. The only way that injustice can cease in the world is for people to know that their true identity is as vast and infinite as Existence itself and is not dependent on the social and cultural dictates of their environment. If you look into the lives of the wealthiest or most powerful people, you will see that the more they have, the more they want. Human appetite is essentially insatiable.

When human beings are driven by their natural appetites, they become dependent on them and inflict injustice on themselves and others. When people come to know their true state of being, their dependencies are transformed and modified. If people were not driven by their appetites, the face of human history would change from one of violence and injustice to one of freedom and peace.

If each human being's goal in life would be to attain his or her true state of dignity and divinity, would there be injustice in the world? If people realized that their identities do not depend on how many credentials they have, or how much money or power or what positions they have, but that their true identity is one and the same as God, would such people be greedy for money, power and position? When all the wealth in the world is yours, do you hoard it or do you share it? When everything is yours, is there anything left to want? When you are fulfilled, is there anything left to desire? This state in Sufism is called *faqr* (poverty). It is a state where greed and need have been transformed into abundance and fulfillment. It is the state of total love, because the individual self has dissolved into the very source of love---God. Sufism is a discipline that transforms people from their base state to their most elevated state.

Just as the sun shines for all equally, the grace of God is present equally for everyone. This is the law. Just as it is the nature of the sun to give, because it is luminous in its own being, so is God's abundance and grace. It is not God who is unjust, because it is in each person's power to decide how much of that knowledge and abundance he or she wants.

At the end of one of my lectures, a young man came up to me and said, "I want to be your *murid* (disciple), I want to follow you." I said, "My entire talk was about not following anyone, about self-discovery, now you say that you want to follow me. First of all, this is against everything I believe and teach. Secondly, it will be a disservice to yourself." I said, "How do you know who I am, that you want to follow me? You've heard me speak and you've liked what I said. Perhaps it was novel and interesting. Tomorrow you may hear someone else and you will want to follow him. Religion is about certainty, and certainty comes when it is grounded in knowledge that has been revealed to you by God, and no one else." I said, "This is a School of Self-Knowledge. It isn't about following someone blindly because you think he looks spiritual or speaks well. I don't teach people to be followers, but to be masters of themselves." I told him that there are plenty of places where people engage in ritualistic practices and they are content with that. In the School of Sufism, everything is focused on discovering "Reality."

Whoever comes to the School is given the prayer of Imam Ja'far al-Sadiq (peace be upon him), the sixth Imam of Shi'a. They are asked to say the prayer in earnest, with an open heart and mind so that God may show them the right path.

> O' God, reveal Yourself to me, for if You do not reveal Yourself to me, I will not know Your Prophet. O' God, if You do not reveal Your Prophet to me, I will not know Your Sign. O' God, reveal Your Sign to me, for if You do not reveal Your Sign to me, I will be misled by my religion.

I gave the young man the prayer and then said to him, "Come back when God has shown you for certain that I have something to offer you." I did not see him for quite a while. One evening he came to one of the gatherings we have in California and afterwards asked if he could speak with me. He came up to me and lowered his head and in a quiet voice said, "Please show me the way to know myself."

It is important that we remember that freedom is not something that can be given to us, but rather it is a state we must create for ourselves, no matter where or who we are. Freedom exists where knowledge exists.

The future is not something one travels to, but it is something that one must build.

ENDNOTES

[1] For an introduction to the works of Spinoza, the reader is referred to Karl Jasper's book entitled *Spinoza*, from the Great Philosophers: The Original Thinkers series edited by Hannah Arendt and translated by Ralph Mannheim, New York: Harcourt Brace and Jovanovich, 1974.

[2] The conventional Arabic transliteration is *Uwais al-Qarani.*

[3] Shah Maghsoud Sadegh Angha, *The Hidden Angles of Life.* Pomana, CA: Multidisciplinary Publications, 1975. The quote here is from a revision in preparation, p. 56.

[4] Shearer, A. and P. Russell, trans. *The Upanishads.* New York: Harper Colophon Books, 1978, p. 15.

[5] Lao Tsu, *Tao Te Ching.* New York: Vintage Books, 1972. Chapter One. Translated by Gia-Fu Feng and Jane English.,

[6] Paul Davies, *Other Worlds.* New York: Simon and Schuster, 1980, pp.12-3.

[7] David Bohm, *Wholeness and the Implicate Order.* London: Routledge & Kegan Paul, 1982.

[8] Karl Pribram interviews in *Psychology Today*, February, 1979, pp.71-84 and *Omni*, October, 1982, pp.129-176

[9] Farid al-Din Attar, *Muslim Saints and Mystics,* transl. A.J. Arberry. London: Routledge & Kegan Paul Ltd. 1983, p.267.

[10] The fourth Sufi Master in the Maktab Tarighe Oveyssi.

[11] Attar, *Muslim Saints and Mystics*, p.63.

[12] James, William, *The Principles of Psychology (2 Volumes).* New York: Holt, Rhineholt, and Winston, 1980. Unaltered republication, New York, Dover, 1950, Volume 1, p. 402.

[13] Grube, G.M.A., trans. *The Republic of Plato.* Indianapolis: Hackett, 1974, pp. 170-1.

[14] Aldous Huxley, *The Human Situation.* Great Britain: Triad Granada, 1980, p.172.

[15] Robert Ornstein quote from Philip Hilts, *Memory Ghost: The Strange Tale of Mr. M and the Nature of Memory*, New York: Simon and Schuster, 1995, p.222.

[16] Philip Hilts, *Memory's Ghost: The Strange Tale of Mr. M and the Nature of Memory.* New York: Simon and Schuster, 1995, p.122.

[17] Sir Arthur Eddington, *The Nature of the Physical World*. New York: MacMillan, 1929. Quoted from Ken Weber's book, *Quantum Questions: Mystical Writings of the World's Greatest Physicists*. Boulder, CO: Shambhala, 1984, p.9.

[18] Special issue of *Scientific American*, entitled *"Life in the Universe."* October 1994. Includes articles by Carl Sagan (*The Search for Extraterrestrial Life*) and Stephen Jay Gould (*The Evolution of Life on the Earth*). Quotes from p.94 and p.86 respectively.

[19] Bohm, David. *op cit.* p. 167.

[20] Karl Pribram interview in *Omni*, October, 1982, p.172.

[21] Pribram, ibid, p. 172.

[22] Pribram, Karl. o*p. cit.*, 1979, p. 84.

[23] David Bohm, *op. cit.*, p.29

[24] Karl Pribram, *op.cit.*, 1982, p.174

[25] David Bohm, *op.cit.*, p.212-3.

[26] Molana Shah Maghsoud Sadegh Angha, *Al Rasa'el*. Lanham: University Press of America, 1986, p.42.

[27] James M. Robinson, ed., *The Nag Hammadi Library* (Translated by members of the Coptic Gnostic Library Project of the Institute for Antiquity and Christianity). New York: Harper and Row, 1977, pp120, 17.

[28] Persian adjective, based on the Arabic proper name, Adam, literally "pertaining to Adam," with the common meaning "humanity." In Persian mystical literature the term signifies the quintessential positive attribute of the concept "humanity," or "humanness."

[29] *Al-Rasa'el*, p.38.

[30] *Al-Rasa'el*, p.38-39.

[31] Molana Shah Maghsoud Sadegh Angha, "Message from the Soul," reprinted in idem., *The Mystery of Humanity: Survival and Tranquillity*. Lanham: University Press of America, 1996, pp. 63-64.

[32] *Al-Rasa'el*, p.13

[33] Karl Jaspers, *op.cit.*, pp.42, 61.

[34] Carl Jung, *Letters, Vol II 1951-1961*. (G. Adler, ed.), Princeton, NJ: Princeton University Press, 1975, pp.194-5.

[35] James Robinson, *op. cit.*, p. 126.

Genealogy of Maktab Tarighat Oveyssi Shahmaghsoudi
(School of Islamic Sufism)®

	Prophet Mohammad
	Imam Ali
1.	Hazrat Oveys Gharani*
2.	Hazrat Salman Farsi
3.	Hazrat Habib-ibn Salim Ra'i
4.	Hazrat Soltan Ebrahim Adham
5.	Hazrat Abu Ali Shaqiq al-Balkhi
6.	Hazrat Sheikh Abu Torab Nakhshabi
7.	Hazrat Sheikh Abi Amr al-Istakhri
8.	Hazrat Abu Ja'far Hazza
9.	Hazrat Sheikh Kabir Abu Abdollah Mohammad-ibn Khafif Shirazi
10.	Hazrat Sheikh Hossein Akkar
11.	Hazrat Sheikh Morshed Abu-Isshaq Shahriar Kazerouni
12.	Hazrat Khatib Abolfath Abdolkarim
13.	Hazrat Ali-ibn Hassan Basri
14.	Hazrat Serajeddin Abolfath Mahmoud-ibn Mahmoudi Sabouni Beyzavi
15.	Hazrat Sheikh Abu Abdollah Rouzbehan Baghli Shirazi
16.	Hazrat Sheikh Najmeddin Tamat-al Kobra Khivaghi
17.	Hazrat Sheikh Ali Lala Ghaznavi
18.	Hazrat Sheikh Ahmad Zaker Jowzeghani
19.	Hazrat Noureddin Abdolrahman Esfarayeni
20.	Hazrat Sheikh Alaoddowleh Semnani
21.	Hazrat Mahmoud Mazdaghani
22.	Hazrat Amir Seyyed Ali Hamedani
23.	Hazrat Sheikh Ahmad Khatlani
24.	Hazrat Seyyed Mohammad Abdollah Ghatifi al-Hasavi Nourbakhsh
25.	Hazrat Shah Ghassem Feyzbakhsh
26.	Hazrat Hossein Abarghoui Janbakhsh
27.	Hazrat Darvish Malek Ali Joveyni
28.	Hazrat Darvish Ali Sodeyri
29.	Hazrat Darvish Kamaleddin Sodeyri
30.	Hazrat Darvish Mohammad Mozaheb Karandehi (Pir Palandouz)
31.	Hazrat Mir Mohammad Mo'men Sodeyri Sabzevari
32.	Hazrat Mir Mohammad Taghi Shahi Mashhadi
33.	Hazrat Mir Mozaffar Ali
34.	Hazrat Mir Mohammad Ali
35.	Hazrat Seyyed Shamseddin Mohammad
36.	Hazrat Seyyed Abdolvahab Naini
37.	Hazrat Haj Mohammad Hassan Kouzekanani
38.	Hazrat Agha Abdolghader Jahromi
39.	Hazrat Jalaleddin Ali Mir Abolfazl Angha
40.	Hazrat Mir Ghotbeddin Mohammad Angha
41.	Hazrat Molana Shah Maghsoud Sadegh Angha
42.	Hazrat Salaheddin Ali Nader Shah Angha

The conventional Arabic transliteration is Uways al-Qarani